21st Century Junior Library

Stegosaurus

by Lucia Raatma

CHERRY LAKE PUBLISHING * ANN ARBOR, MICHIGAN

CHERRY LAKE Publishing

Published in the United States of America by Cherry Lake Publishing
Ann Arbor, Michigan
www.cherrylakepublishing.com

Content Adviser: Gregory M. Erickson, PhD, Dinosaur Paleontologist, Department of
Biological Science, Florida State University, Tallahassee, Florida

Reading Adviser: Marla Conn, Read with Me Now

Photo Credits: Cover, ©musk/Alamy; page 4, ©iStockphoto.com/danku; page 6, ©SPY0013215/
Media Bakery; pages 8 and 18, ©Catmando/Shutterstock, Inc.; page 10, ©Stocktrek Images, Inc./
Alamy; page 12, ©Linda Bucklin/Shutterstock, Inc.; page 14, ©Jean-Michel Girard/Shutterstock, Inc.;
page 16, ©STT0008143/Media Bakery; page 20, ©ZUMA Wire Service/Alamy

LIBRARY OF CONGRESS CATALOGING-IN-PUBLICATION DATA
Raatma, Lucia.
  Stegosaurus/by Lucia Raatma.
     p. cm.—(21st century junior library dinosaurs)
  Includes bibliographical references and index.
  ISBN 978-1-61080-465-3 (lib. bdg.)—ISBN 978-1-61080-552-0 (e-book)—
ISBN 978-1-61080-639-8 (pbk.)
  1. Stegosaurus—Juvenile literature. I. Title.
  QE862.O65R33 2013
  567.915'3—dc23   2012003548

Cherry Lake Publishing would like to acknowledge the work of
The Partnership for 21st Century Skills.
Please visit www.21stcenturyskills.org *for more information.*

Printed in the United States of America
Corporate Graphics Inc.
July 2012
CLFA11

CONTENTS

Many scientists believe *Stegosauruses*
lived in groups.

What Was a *Stegosaurus*?

Picture a dinosaur with huge plates on its back. That would be the *Stegosaurus*. It looked like no other dinosaur. The *Stegosaurus* lived about 150 million years ago. But like all other dinosaurs, the *Stegosaurus* is now **extinct**.

A *Stegosaurus* can be recognized
by the plates on its back.

Where did the name *Stegosaurus* come from? It is a Greek word that means "roofed lizard." Scientists named the dinosaur for the triangular plates along its back. The *Stegosaurus* lived in North America and parts of Europe. Close relatives of these dinosaurs lived all over the world.

Think! What other animals are covered with hard scales or plates? What are these body parts used for?

Scientists have argued about how plates were positioned on a *Stegosaurus*'s back.

What Did a *Stegosaurus* Look Like?

The *Stegosaurus* is best known for its plates. The large, flat, triangle-shaped plates were arranged in two rows. The dinosaur also had bony **scutes**. These were located on the sides of its neck and around its hips. They were similar to the bumps on an alligator's back.

The *Stegosaurus* could use its spiked
tail to fight predators.

The *Stegosaurus* had an amazing tail! It was long and flexible, with four spikes on the end. Each spike was as long as 4 feet (1.2 meters). They may have helped the dinosaur protect itself from **predators**.

A *Stegosaurus* was almost as long as
a school bus.

A *Stegosaurus* could be 26 to 30 feet (8 to 9 m) long. It was about 9 feet (2.7 m) tall. It weighed nearly 6,000 pounds (2,722 kilograms). That's as heavy as a large SUV or pickup truck!

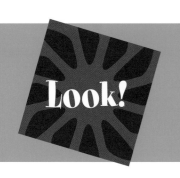

Look!

The next time you are in a parking lot, look at all the cars. Imagine if they were all dinosaurs! Which ones look like a *Stegosaurus*?

The *Stegosaurus*'s brain was tiny for an
animal of its size.

This dinosaur also had strong, thick legs. Its front feet had five short toes. These toes looked like **hooves**. Its back feet had three toes. Though its body was huge, the *Stegosaurus*'s head was small. Its brain was only as big as a tennis ball!

Create!

Draw a picture of a tennis ball. Think about how small it is. Now draw pictures of other items about the same size. Consider a baseball or a few walnuts. Can you believe that the *Stegosaurus* had a brain that small?

The *Stegosaurus* might have been able
to stand on its back legs to reach high leaves.

How Did a *Stegosaurus* Live?

The *Stegosaurus* did not eat meat. It was an **herbivore**. It ate bushes, leaves, and ferns. Some scientists think it could only eat low-growing plants. Other scientists disagree. They think the dinosaur may have reared up on its back legs. Then it could reach higher branches.

Some scientists believe that plate colors helped
Stegosauruses tell each other apart.

Scientists are not sure what the *Stegosaurus*'s plates were for. Some think the plates helped control the dinosaur's body temperature. Plate colors and shapes might have helped identify different kinds of *Stegosaurus*. Modern-day birds often use color the same way.

Ask Questions!

Talk to your friends and family. When they are warm, how do they cool off? When they are cold, what heats them up?

A visitor can see *Stegosaurus* and other fossils at museums around the world.

How have scientists learned about the *Stegosaurus*? They have discovered **fossils** and studied them. Some fossils have been found in Colorado and Utah in the United States. There is so much we can learn from dinosaur fossils!

Make a Guess!

How hard is it for scientists to piece fossils together? How do you think they start the process? Ask a teacher, librarian, or other adult for help finding the answers.

GLOSSARY

extinct (ek-STINGKT) describing a type of plant or animal that has completely died out

fossils (FAH-suhlz) the preserved remains of living things from thousands or millions of years ago

herbivore (HUR-buh-vor) an animal that eats plants rather than other animals

hooves (HOOVZ) the hard coverings over the toes of horses or deer

predators (PRED-uh-turz) animals that live by hunting other animals for food

scutes (SKYOOTS) very large scales on a reptile that often have bone plates underneath that serve as armor

FIND OUT MORE

BOOKS

Gray, Susan Heinrichs. *Stegosaurus*. Mankato, MN: The Child's World, 2010.

Mara, Wil. *Stegosaurus*. New York: Children's Press, 2012.

WEB SITES

American Museum of Natural History: Stegosaurus
www.amnh.org/exhibitions/ expeditions/treasure_fossil/Fossils/ Specimens/stegosaurus.html
Learn more about *Stegosaurus* and see a photo of a fossil.

Denver Museum of Nature & Science: Prehistoric Journey
www.dmns.org/exhibitions/current -exhibitions/prehistoric-journey
Travel through time and watch *Stegosaurus* in action.

INDEX

ABOUT THE AUTHOR

Lucia Raatma has written dozens of books for young readers. She and her family live in the Tampa Bay area of Florida. They enjoy looking at the dinosaur fossils at the local science museum.